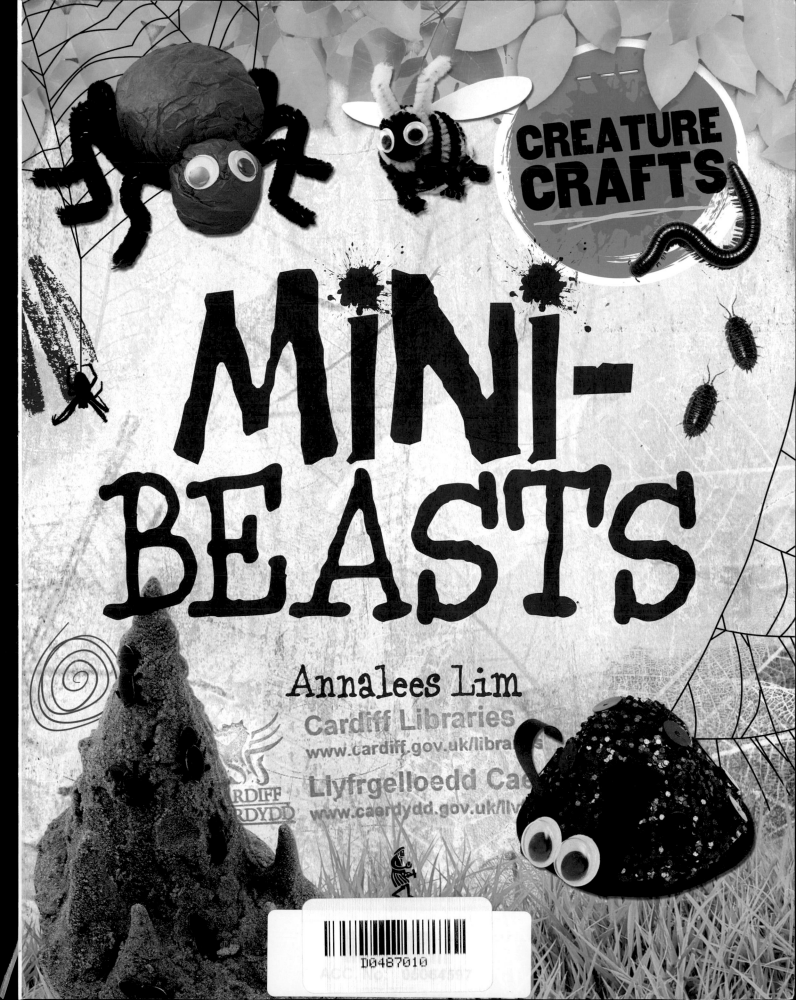

CREATURE CRAFTS

MINI-BEASTS

Annalees Lim

CONTENTS

Welcome to the world of minibeasts!

Are minibeasts your favourite animals? Would you like to make some of your own and find out loads of fun facts about them along the way? Then this book is for you! Follow the step-by-step instructions on each page to craft termites, dragonflies, spiders and much more.

A lot of the projects use paint and PVA glue. Always cover surfaces with a piece of plastic or layers of old newspaper. Whenever you can, leave the project to dry before moving on to the next step. This avoids things getting stuck to each other or paint smudging.

So, do you have your craft tools at the ready? Then get set to make your craft creepy-crawlies and discover what makes each of them so special!

SPARKLY LADYBIRD

Ladybirds have brightly coloured, hard wing cases that protect their folded wings. This ladybird's wing cases are covered in glitter so they shimmer and sparkle!

1 Use the scissors to cut out an egg box section. It should be about 4cm high.

2 Cover the egg box section in PVA glue and sprinkle red glitter all over it. Leave to dry.

3

Use a compass to measure a circle of black card that is a bit bigger than the base of the egg box section. It should be about 5cm wide. Cut this out.

4

Cut out 2 thin strips of black card that are 4cm long. Stick these onto the black circle and curl the ends using your pencil.

5

Stick your egg box section onto the black card circle using the PVA glue. Use the glue to attach the black sequins that make the ladybird spots. Glue on the googly eyes.

LADYBIRD FACT

The bright colour and spots on a ladybird's wing cases are a warning to birds: they tell birds that they shouldn't eat this animal because it tastes nasty.

SNAiL STAMP

You will need:
10cm x 10cm of thick card
PVA glue
Ball of string
Paint and paintbrush
A4 light blue card
A4 green paper
Coloured paper
White paper
Scissors
Glue stick
Sticky tape
Googly eyes
Tape measure

Did you know that no two snail shells are the same? Create your own unique snails with this crafty shell stamp!

1

Cut 3 lengths of string that are each 50cm long. Use some sticky tape to join them together at one end. Plait the strings and use sticky tape to fix their ends together.

2

Tape the plait to the middle of the card square. Carefully cover the rest of the card with a layer of PVA glue.

3

Stick the string onto the card in a spiral shape. Make sure you keep the string as flat as possible. Leave this stamp to dry before using it in Step 5.

4

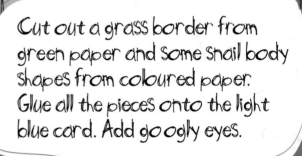

Cut out a grass border from green paper and some snail body shapes from coloured paper. Glue all the pieces onto the light blue card. Add googly eyes.

5

Cover the stamp with paint. Place it on white paper and press down firmly. Lift off the stamp to reveal your print. Cut out the print and glue it to a snail body.

SNAIL FACT
Snails can seal themselves into their shells and stay there for months! They do this if the weather is too hot and dry for them.

SPIDERS IN A WEB

Spiders create webs to catch food. Weave your very own sparkly spider's web and craft some googly-eyed spiders, too!

1

Scrunch up 2 A4-sized pieces of tissue paper into a ball. Do the same with an A5-sized piece of tissue paper. Glue both balls together to make the spider body and head.

2

Cut 2 pipe cleaners in half and twist all 4 pieces together. Bend the ends of the pipe cleaners into leg shapes and glue them to the body.

3

Repeat steps 1 and 2 with different coloured tissue paper. Stick googly eyes on each spider.

4

Starting in the middle of the purple card, sew a star shape into the card using the silver embroidery thread. Ask an adult to help you.

5

Start in the centre of the star you have stitched and use the embroidery thread to weave a coil shape onto it. Place your spiders on their web!

SPIDER FACT

The silk that spiders make to weave their webs is finer than our hair, but it is stronger than steel!

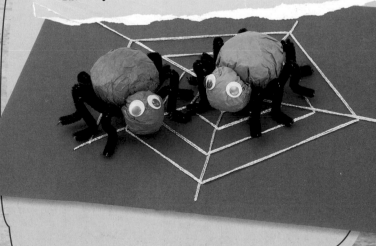

BUTTERFLY PAPER CHAIN

Butterflies have four brightly coloured wings. Create a chain of butterflies with colourful wings to decorate your room!

1

Cut 3 paper strips so that one is 20cm long, one is 16cm long and one is 12cm long. Staple them all together at one end.

2

Bend the paper strips so that the ends all line up, without making a crease in the paper. Staple them together. Repeat steps 1 and 2.

3

Make 2 smaller shapes in the same way as in steps 1 and 2, but use strips that are 15cm, 11cm and 9cm long.

4

Use sticky tape to join all the paper shapes to make a butterfly.

5

Make as many butterflies as you want in the chain. Join them all together by stapling the top wings to each other. Tie a piece of ribbon to each end of the chain to hang it up.

BUTTERFLY FACT
Did you know that butterflies taste with their feet? Their sense of taste is 200 times stronger than ours!

SHINY DRAGONFLY

You will need:
- Flat kitchen sponges
- Metallic paint
- Gold paint
- Scissors
- PVA glue
- Paintbrush
- Wooden clothes peg
- Thin black marker pen

Dragonflies are some of the fastest fliers in the minibeast world! Craft yours with wings that shimmer and glisten in the Sun.

1

Paint 2 sponges with a layer of metallic paint. Remember to leave the sponges to dry before painting the other side.

2

Paint the wooden clothes peg gold and leave to dry.

3

Cut out 4 long, thin ovals for the wings, a log, thin shape for the body, and a circle for the head. Cut out 5 small rectangles.

4

Use a marker pen to draw the veins of the wings onto each oval.

5

Glue the head and body onto the peg, and decorate with small rectangles. Glue the wings onto the body and leave your dragonfly upside down to dry.

DRAGONFLY FACT

Did you know that dragonflies catch their food with their feet? They only eat prey that they have caught in flight.

JEWEL BUG

Jewel bugs are some of the most colourful minibeasts in the world! Use this fun sgraffito method to make your own gem-like creepy-crawlies.

1

Colour white card in with blue, green and red crayons.

2

Cover all of your crayon markings with black crayon.

3

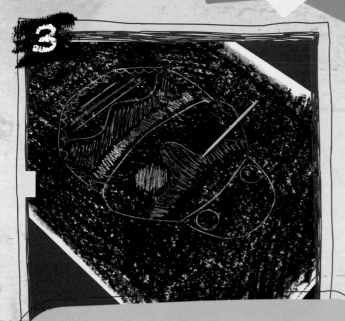

Use a tooth pick to Scratch off the black crayon layer in the Shape of a bug body and head. Cut your bug out. Scratch off patterns, too.

4

Cut out leaf shapes from green paper. Use a green felt tip pen to draw leaf veins onto them. Glue the leaves to a piece of white A4 card.

5

Cut your bug out and glue it onto the leafy background. Draw the legs and the antennae on with a black marker.

JEWEL BUG FACT
Some jewel bugs are not only colourful, they even look shiny and metallic!

TERMITE MOUND

You will need:
Sand
A small and a large paper pulp seedling pot
PVA glue
Thick card
Pumpkin seeds
Scissors
Black and brown paint
Paintbrushes

Some termites build homes, called mounds, which can be up to 9 metres high! The mound for your crafty colony of termites can be much smaller.

1

Cut thick card into a wavy shape. Stack your seedling pots and stick them upside down onto the shape using PVA glue.

2

Cover everything in a layer of PVA and sprinkle sand over the top. Shake off the excess sand and leave to dry.

Mix the sand with PVA glue and use the mixture to build litte turrets. Place them around the mound.

Glue one and a half pumpkin seeds together onto the sand to make the head and body of a termite. You can create a colony by adding many more.

Paint each termite brown. Then draw their legs onto the sand using black paint.

TERMITE FACT

A lot of termites are born blind. They spend most of their lives inside the dark mound.

BUMBLE BEES

Bumble bees look a bit like honey bees, but they are bigger and fluffier. Follow these steps to make fuzzy bumble bees using pipe cleaners!

You will need:
2 black and 2 yellow pipe cleaners
Thick plastic, such as acetate sheets
Scissors
Googly eyes
Fabric glue
Pencil
Ruler

1

Twist a black and a yellow pipe cleaner together at one end, so they are joined.

2

Start wrapping the pipe cleaners around your thumb. Finish by pulling your thumb out and pushing the ends of the pipe cleaners into the hole where your thumb was.

3

Draw 2 wing shapes on a plastic sheet and cut them out. Stick these wings to the body using fabric glue.

4

Cut 6 lengths of black pipe cleaner that are 3cm long. Bend them into leg shapes and stick them under the body.

5

Cut 2 short pieces of yellow pipe cleaner and stick them into the head to make antennae. Glue some googly eyes onto the bumble bee's face.

BUMBLE BEE FACT

Bumble bees only make enough honey to feed their young. The honey we eat comes from honey bees.

PRAYING MANTIS

A praying mantis is hard to spot because it looks like the twigs and leaves it lives on. Make your own praying mantis to hide in plants around your home!

1

Cut 2 bendy straws to be 9cm long. Place them onto the outside prongs of a plastic fork and bend them back.

2

Draw a face shape and eyes on green foam with a black marker pen. Cut out the face.

3

Tape the foam face onto the antennae. Wrap the whole fork in green electrical tape.

4

Wrap pipe cleaners around the head, middle and bottom, twisting them into place. Bend them into leg shapes to make your praying mantis stand up.

5

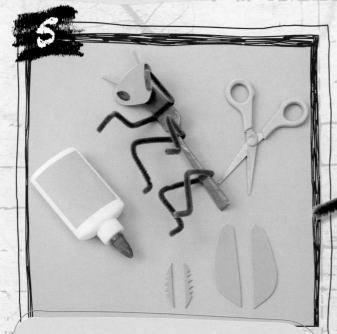

Cut out foam shapes for the front legs and the back of the body. Glue them in place using PVA glue.

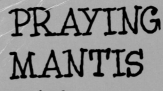

PRAYING MANTIS FACT

This minibeast is called praying mantis because it often folds its front legs into a praying position.

CATERPILLAR COLLAGE

You will need:
Lots of coloured, patterned paper
Scissors
Glue stick
2 sheets of A4 green card
Pencil
Black pen
Googly eyes
Compass

Caterpillars come in many different sizes and colours. Choose lots of coloured, patterned paper to create your caterpillar collage!

1

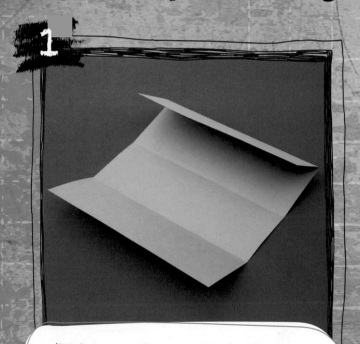

Fold green A4 card in half, open it up and fold each side into the middle. Open up so you have 3 folds in the card. Number them 1–3, from left to right.

2

Fold the left hand side so that it lines up with fold 3. Open it up again. Fold the right hand side so that it lines up with fold 1 and open it up again.

3

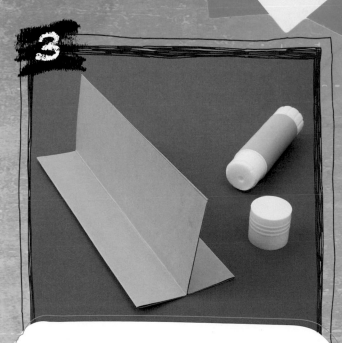

Fold the paper using the creases to create a 'T' shape. Glue the folds into place.

4

Cut the short edge of a sheet of A4 green card to look like grass. Fold it and stick it to the T-shaped card.

5

Cut out lots of circles from colourful paper. Stick them onto the green card in the shape of a caterpillar. Draw its legs in black pen and stick on googly eyes. You can add 2 strips of paper to make antennae!

CATERPILLAR FACT

Did you know that caterpillars live for about a week before they start to turn into butterflies?

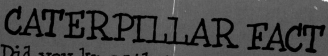

GLOSSARY

colony	a big group of animals that lives together
gem	a stone that is often shiny and is very precious
metallic	when something looks like metal
prey	the animal that another animal hunts for food
seal	to lock something away
sgraffito	a craft that is made by scratching away a layer of colour to show other colours underneath
steel	a strong metal that is used to build skyscrapers
unique	when something is one of a kind, not like anything else

INDEX

Published in paperback in 2016

Copyright © Hodder & Stoughton Limited 2016

Wayland
Carmelite House, 50 Victoria Embankment,
London EC4Y 0DZ

All rights reserved.

Wayland, part of Hachette Children's Group and published by Hodder and Stoughton Limited
www.hachette.co.uk

Series editor: Julia Adams
Craft photography: Simon Pask, N1 Studios
Additional images: Shutterstock

ISBN: 9780750297196
ebook ISBN: 9780750293778

Printed in China

MIX
Paper from responsible sources
FSC
www.fsc.org
FSC® C104740